LOVE WAS CHEAP and LIFE WAS HIGH

Postcards from
Paperback Cover Art
of the 40s and 50s

EDITED BY
BARRY JAY KAPLAN

Collier Books • Macmillan Publishing Company • New York

Collier Macmillan Canada • Toronto   Maxwell Macmillan International • New York • Oxford • Singapore • Sydney

Collier Books   Collier Macmillan Canada, Inc.
Macmillan Publishing Company   1200 Eglinton Avenue East, Suite 200
866 Third Avenue, New York, NY 10022   Don Mills, Ontario M3C 3N1

Library of Congress Cataloging-in-Publication Data

Love was cheap and life was high: postcards from paperback cover art
of the 40s and 50s/edited by Barry Jay Kaplan.
    p.   cm.
    ISBN 0-02-033987-9
    1. Book covers—United States.   2. Paperbacks—United States—
Illustrations.   3. United States—Popular culture.   I. Kaplan,
Barry Jay.
NC973.5.U6L68   1990
741.6'4'09730904—dc20   90-1838
                                                          CIP

Design by Ellen R. Sasahara

10 9 8 7 6 5 4 3 2 1

PRINTED IN SINGAPORE

NOTE: Because these postcards are oversized, they need the same postage as a first-class letter.

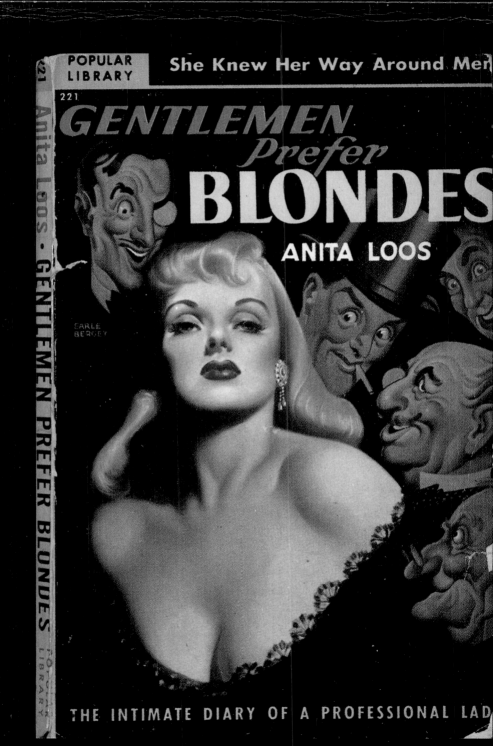

221

She Knew Her Way Around Men

GENTLEMEN
Prefer
BLONDES

ANITA LOOS

EARLE
BERGEY

THE INTIMATE DIARY OF A PROFESSIONAL LAD

LOVE WAS CHEAP AND LIFE WAS HIGH • Collier Books
Copyright © 1990 by Barry Jay Kaplan

Gentlemen Prefer Blondes by Anita Loos. Published by Popular Library in 1949. Originally published by *Harper's Bazaar* in 1925. Cover art by Earle Bergey, whose stunning image of Lorelei Lee was superseded forever by the movie's version: Marilyn Monroe. "Lorelei Lee was a cute number with lots of sex appeal and the ability to make it pay off. None of the men who crossed her path was ever the same again." A few years ago, *The New York Times* called the book a neglected masterpiece.

LOVE WAS CHEAP AND LIFE WAS HIGH • Collier Books
Copyright © 1990 by Barry Jay Kaplan

Death in the Library by Philip Ketchum. Published by the new Dell Publishing Company in 1943. Originally published in hardcover by Crowell. Cover artist unknown. Each book in this Dell "Keyhole" Series included a cast of characters and a list entitled "Things this Mystery is about—'' "A disturbing letter. A suicide note. The fallen book. Cancelled checks. The key in the old cigar box. Capsules within capsules. The missing gun. And a private investigator on a personal prowl."

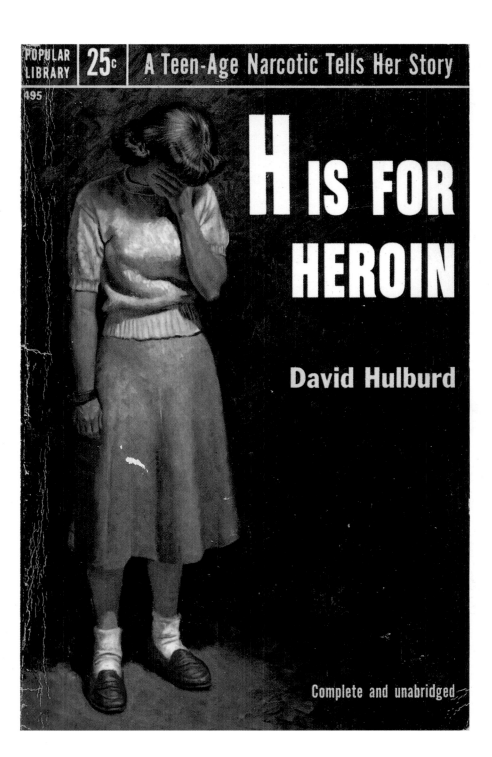

LOVE WAS CHEAP AND LIFE WAS HIGH • Collier Books
Copyright © 1990 by Barry Jay Kaplan

H is for Heroin by David Hulburd. Published by Popular Library in 1953. Originally published in hardcover by Doubleday. Cover art by Rafael de Soto. The realism of the cover painting was an attempt to deal seriously and unglamorously with teenage addiction. "Dope always gives you a raw deal. Take it from Amy Burton, only seventeen and married to a boy who gave her heroin. Like most of her teenage pals, she was hooked. This is her story . . . and it's not a pretty one."

LOVE WAS CHEAP AND LIFE WAS HIGH • Collier Books
Copyright © 1990 by Barry Jay Kaplan

Home to Harlem by Claude McKay. Published by Avon Books in 1951. Originally published in hardcover by Harper and Brothers in 1928. Cover art by Ray Johnson, portraying "a symbolic panorama of the people and places we meet in the vivid pages to come: brown girls rouged and painted like dark posies. Tan flesh draped in soft clinging silk. Full red lips pouted for sweet kissing. Brown bosoms throbbing with love."

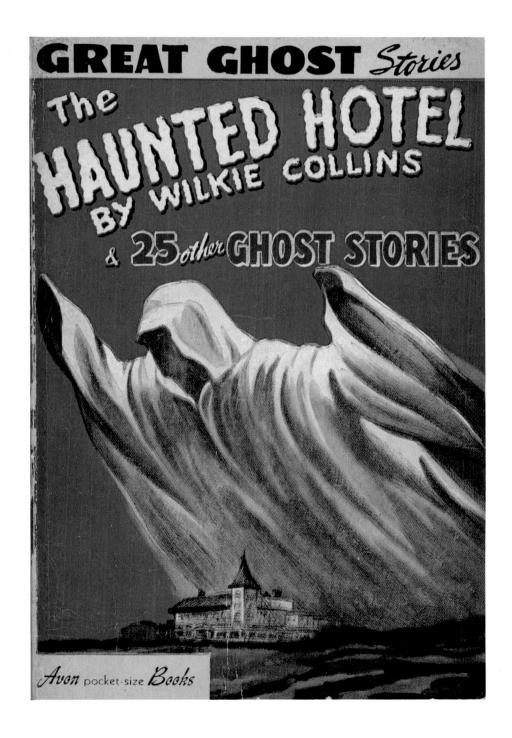

LOVE WAS CHEAP AND LIFE WAS HIGH • Collier Books
Copyright © 1990 by Barry Jay Kaplan

The Haunted Hotel. An original anthology of twenty-five ghost stories. Published by Avon Books in 1941. Cover artist unknown. This volume was Avon's sixth and its first collection. It contained stories by Wilkie Collins, Poe, de Maupassant, S. Baring-Gould and others, cryptically, by A Lady, A Constabulary Officer, A Witness, A Sportsman, A Traveler and A Spinster.

JOHN O'HARA
BUtterfield 8

LOVE WAS CHEAP AND LIFE WAS HIGH • Collier Books
Copyright © 1990 by Barry Jay Kaplan

Butterfield 8 by John O'Hara. Published by Avon Books in 1946. Originally published in hardcover by Harcourt, Brace in 1935. Cover artist unknown. BU8- became the most famous telephone exchange in literature. "Corrupted early by a lecherous uncle, she grew to young womanhood with a sure knowledge of what men wanted . . . and a sophisitcated view of the passions that seemed to pay off in jewels, mink coats and a fast-paced life of dangerous pleasures in New York's most luxurious love-nests."

BY THE AUTHOR OF "The BRIDGE of SAN LUIS REY"

Heaven's My Destination

THORNTON WILDER

AN AVON BOOK

LOVE WAS CHEAP AND LIFE WAS HIGH • Collier Books
Copyright © 1990 by Barry Jay Kaplan

Heaven's My Destination by Thornton Wilder. Published by Avon Books in 1945. Originally published in hardcover by Harper and Brothers in 1935. Cover artist unknown. Wilder was already famous for *The Bridge of San Luis Rey.* His new book, the adventures of a traveling salesman and religious convert, took its title from a doggerel verse children of the Middle West were accustomed to write in their schoolbooks: "George Brush is my name;/America's my nation;/Luddington's my dwelling-place/And Heaven's my destination."

NO ONE ON BANNER STREET COULD BREAK THE
STRANGLEHOLD THAT BOUND THEM TO POVERTY AND VICE

TOUGH KID

FROM
BROOKLYN

(*SPIT AND THE STARS*)

382
AVON
POCKET-SIZE BOOKS

ANC

LOVE WAS CHEAP AND LIFE WAS HIGH • Collier Books
Copyright © 1990 by Barry Jay Kaplan

Tough Kid From Brooklyn by Robert Mende. Published by Avon Books in 1951. Cover artist unknown. The cover is meant to be a sympathetic study of Gregg and Dynamite as they wonder about their future. "They meet on the dirty stoops and discuss a world of clean apartments, hot water, enough food—someday, maybe, some-day.... They swear by their fantastic lies to each other, for only in fantasy does their extreme poverty seem lessened. 'It ain't easy to live in a concrete jungle!'"

LOVE WAS CHEAP AND LIFE WAS HIGH • Collier Books

Finger Man and other stories by Raymond Chandler. Published by Avon Books in 1946, with permission from *Black Mask*, *The Atlantic Monthly* and Street & Smith Publications. Cover artist unknown. The cover followed the description in the book, except for the color of her hair and dress. "Here are stories of violence, packed with shapely underworld women whose kisses are blood-red and whose boyfriends serenade them to the sound of barking lead and coughing Tommy-guns."

SHE WAS SEDUCTIVE AND DANGEROUS

TALES OF
Chinatown

SAX ROHMER

Ten stories of macabre mystery by the creator of the famous Dr. Fu Manchu

LOVE WAS CHEAP AND LIFE WAS HIGH • Collier Books
Copyright © 1990 by Barry Jay Kaplan

Tales of Chinatown by Sax Rohmer. Published by Popular Library. Originally published in hardcover by Doubleday, Page in 1922. Cover art by Rudolph Belarski, who, in 1952, had done fifty Popular Library covers. His look influenced the whole line and was widely imitated. The book included ten stories of England's Chinatown, "where life moves in devious paths and the subtle intrigues of the Orient challenge all the resources of New Scotland Yard."

LOVE WAS CHEAP AND LIFE WAS HIGH • Collier Books
Copyright © 1990 by Barry Jay Kaplan

The Phantom of the Opera by Gaston Leroux. Published by Dell in 1943. Cover art by Gerald Gregg. The map on the back cover is a mock architectural rendering of the levels of the Paris Opera House. The covers in Dell's early years are memorable for the brilliance of their four-color printing and the evocative use of the airbrush technique, which accomplished the goal of making all the books in the line stand out in the increasingly competitive paperback-book market.

550

Thomas Wolfe Short Stories

Only The Dead
Know Brooklyn

Selections from "From Death to Morning" plus "The Story of a Novel"

A SIGNET BOOK

LOVE WAS CHEAP AND LIFE WAS HIGH • Collier Books
Copyright © 1990 by Barry Jay Kaplan

Only the Dead Know Brooklyn by Thomas Wolfe. Published by Signet Books in 1947, by arrangement with Charles Scribner's Sons. Cover art by Rudolph Nappi, in the style of James Avati. The collection also includes selections from "The Story of a Novel," but it was the title story that drew people in. "Canarsie. East New York. Flatbush. Bensonhurst. Bay Ridge. Greenpoint. This is the itinerary of a lost man, wandering through the wilds of Brooklyn seeking something he cannot name."

LOVE WAS CHEAP AND LIFE WAS HIGH • Collier Books
Copyright © 1990 by Barry Jay Kaplan

I Was a Nazi Flier by Gottfried Leske. Published by Dell in 1943. Cover artist Gerald Gregg used his signature airbrush technique and one of Dell's most popular cover-design motifs: the grinning skull. The author was said to be a flight sergeant in the *Luftwaffe*. The introduction by Clifton Fadiman assured the reader that what they were about to read was not fiction.

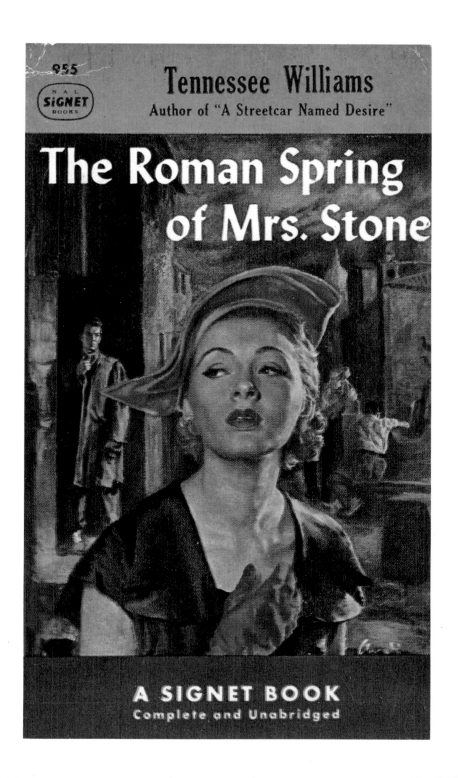

955

Tennessee Williams

Author of "A Streetcar Named Desire"

The Roman Spring of Mrs. Stone

A SIGNET BOOK

Complete and Unabridged

LOVE WAS CHEAP AND LIFE WAS HIGH • Collier Books

The *Roman Spring of Mrs. Stone* by Tennessee Williams. Published by Signet Books in 1952. Originally published in hardcover by New Directions in 1950. Cover art by James Avati, who pioneered a new realism in paperback cover art that matched the maturity of the stories. "Self knowledge was something Karen Stone had been able to avoid until the middle of her life. Then the stream of her life was rudely diverted, carrying her to Europe and to a new kind of existence in the oldest of modern cities—timeless Rome. This novel is the story of her 'Roman Spring,' of her crisis of self-recognition, and the loves which precipitated it."

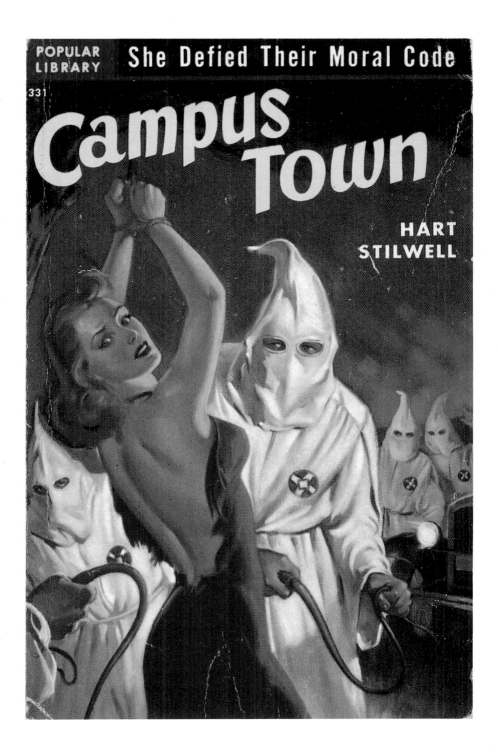

POPULAR LIBRARY

331

She Defied Their Moral Code

Campus Town

HART STILWELL

LOVE WAS CHEAP AND LIFE WAS HIGH • Collier Books
Copyright © 1990 by Barry Jay Kaplan

Campus Town by Hart Stilwell. Published by Popular Library in 1951. Originally published in hardcover by Doubleday in 1950. Cover art by Rudolph Belarski. For paperback collectors, this is one of the most valuable, combining sex, sadism and social comment. "He could still see it all: a man and a woman roped to a tree and surrounded by hooded Klansmen. Then the lash of a whip and a shrill scream as the woman's half-naked body writhed in agony...."

LOVE WAS CHEAP AND LIFE WAS HIGH • Collier Books
Copyright © 1990 by Barry Jay Kaplan

Mosquitoes by William Faulkner. Published by Avon Books in 1941. Originally published in hardcover by Liveright in 1927. "Much promise," said the *Boston Transcript*. "The characters: a social climber and literary lion huntress who collects a famous writer, a sculptor, a sex-innocent idiot, a most modern young lady and a mechanically inclined brother. They almost all come against their better judgments; they all more or less live to regret it."

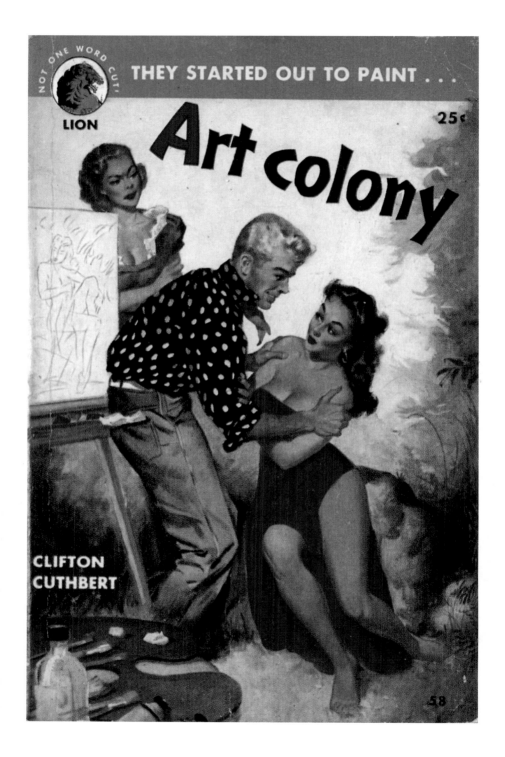

THEY STARTED OUT TO PAINT . . .

25¢

Art colony

CLIFTON
CUTHBERT

58

LOVE WAS CHEAP AND LIFE WAS HIGH • Collier Books
Copyright © 1990 by Barry Jay Kaplan

Art Colony by Clifton Cuthbert. Published by Lion Books in 1951. Originally published in hardcover by William Godwin in 1933. Cover artist unknown. Lion was a small imprint that published between 1949 and 1955, and then it was bought by New American Library. "You might say they went to Woodfay to write or to paint or to do something artistic. You might say it, but nobody who saw them up there would believe you. What they did, some people might call artistic, but others just call it fun."

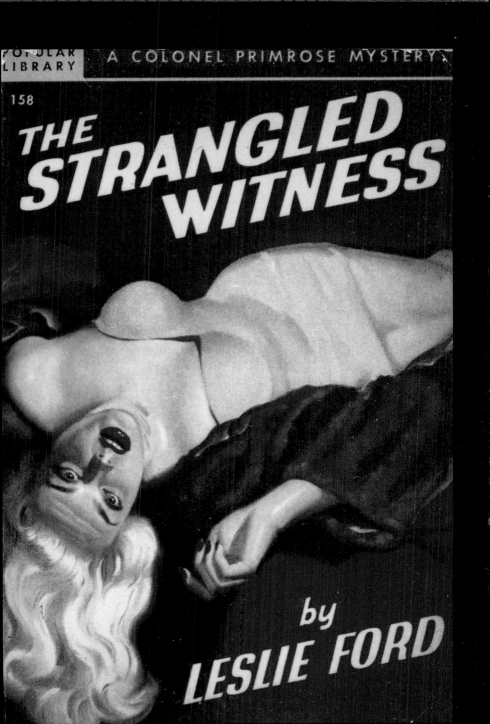

LOVE WAS CHEAP AND LIFE WAS HIGH • Collier Books
Copyright © 1990 by Barry Jay Kaplan

The Strangled Witness by Leslie Ford. Published by Popular Library in 1946. "Books of Proven Merit" appears on all back covers. Originally published in hardcover by Farrar and Rinehart in 1944. Cover art by Rudolph Belarski. An archetypal forties image that shows the influence of film noir: a dead blonde in a low-cut gown and a fur coat. "The case was a stalemate until Colonel Primrose, a sentimental gentleman sleuth, smoked out the killer in this breathless mystery novel of the nation's cosmopolitan capital."

550

MILTON BERLE'S JOKE BOOK

Out of My Trunk

LOVE WAS CHEAP AND LIFE WAS HIGH • Collier Books
Copyright © 1990 by Barry Jay Kaplan

Out of My Trunk by Milton Berle. Published by Bantam Books in 1948. Originally published in hardcover by Grayson Publishing in 1945. Cover artist unknown. The pre-TV Uncle Miltie dedicated the book to his mother, "who never started the applause for me. She just kept it from dying down." An example of Berle's humor: "CO-ED: I want a pair of bloomers to wear around my gymnasium. CLERK: Certainly, miss, what size is your gymnasium?"

937

N·A·L·
SiGNET
BOOKS

Bohemian Life in a Wicked City

Goodbye to Berlin

CHRISTOPHER ISHERWOOD

A SIGNET BOOK
Complete and Unabridged

LOVE WAS CHEAP AND LIFE WAS HIGH • Collier Books

Goodbye to Berlin by Christopher Isherwood. Published by Signet Books in 1952. Originally published in hardcover by New Directions in 1945. Cover art by James Avati, considered by his peers to be the greatest cover artist of them all. His emotional imagery was strongly influenced by films he saw. Here he gives us a very earthy Sally Bowles, complete with green nail polish, just one of the characters living in a city "whose moral values were crumbling" under the pressure of the impending chaos of Nazi oppression.

NEW AVON LIBRARY

THE BIG SLEEP

**RAYMOND
CHANDLER**

AVON

The Big Sleep by Raymond Chandler. Published by Avon Books in 1943. Originally published in hardcover by Knopf in 1939. Cover artist unknown. A mere reference to Avon #38 is enough to set a paperback collector's pulse racing: a classic cover on a classic American novel. In it Philip Marlowe set out to crack a case of blackmail and got in up to his neck in a series of murders. Justice, though of an unexpected sort, is finally done.

A DELL BOOK

DELL

270

IT AIN'T HAY

DAVID DODGE

WITH CRIME MAP ON BACK COVER

A DELL THRILLER

LOVE WAS CHEAP AND LIFE WAS HIGH • Collier Books
Copyright © 1990 by Barry Jay Kaplan

It Ain't Hay by David Dodge. Published by Dell in 1949. Originally published in hardcover by Simon and Schuster in 1946. Cover artist unknown. Part of the Dell MapBack Series—the back is a map of where the action takes place. San Francisco: "Where marijuana and murder make a thrilling story...."

754

N·A·L
SiGNET
BOOKS

KISS TOMORROW GOOD-BYE

HORACE McCOY

SIGNET BOOKS
A Special Edition

LOVE WAS CHEAP AND LIFE WAS HIGH • Collier Books
Copyright © 1990 by Barry Jay Kaplan

Kiss Tomorrow Goodbye by Horace McCoy. Published by Signet Books in 1948. Originally published in hardcover by Random House in 1948. Cover art by James Avati, known for the raw emotion he could pack into a cover. A perfect match for a story about a crime genius and an amoral wench. "They might have made it if it hadn't been for the spoiled daughter of a millionaire, a perfume from the dream-haunted past . . . and a certain bullet."

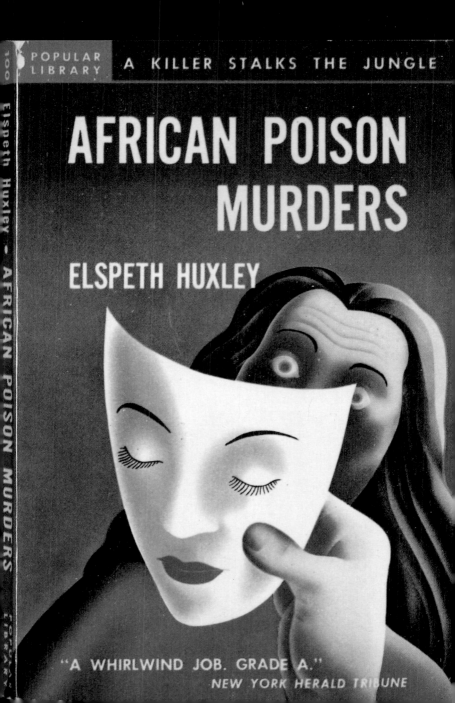

A KILLER STALKS THE JUNGLE

AFRICAN POISON MURDERS

ELSPETH HUXLEY

"A WHIRLWIND JOB. GRADE A."
NEW YORK HERALD TRIBUNE

LOVE WAS CHEAP AND LIFE WAS HIGH • Collier Books

African Poison Murders by Elspeth Huxley. Published by Popular Library in 1946. Originally published in hardcover by Harper and Brothers in 1939. Cover artist unknown. First published in England as *Death of an Aryan*. "Strange things were happening to African East Coast farmers. A native boy was found dead, baling wire embedded in his flesh. The local officer blundered into a leopard trap, a killer in the African dark jabbed a poison-tipped stick at him. There was no antidote to save him. He was at the mercy of an unseen murderer who revelled in torturing his victims."

Musk, hashish and blood

HECTOR FRANCE

★308★
AVON
POCKET-SIZE BOOK
ANC

LOVE WAS CHEAP AND LIFE WAS HIGH • Collier Books
Copyright © 1990 by Barry Jay Kaplan

Musk, Hashish and Blood by Hector France. Published as a paper-back original by Avon Books in 1951. Cover artist unknown, although obviously influenced by Earle Bergey, for whom breasts were a speciality. "Adventure and violence on the grand scale is mingled with the most intimate and poignantly human details of Arab folkways in such fascinating episodes as 'The Bridal of Little Zariah' and 'The Breasts of Meryem.'"

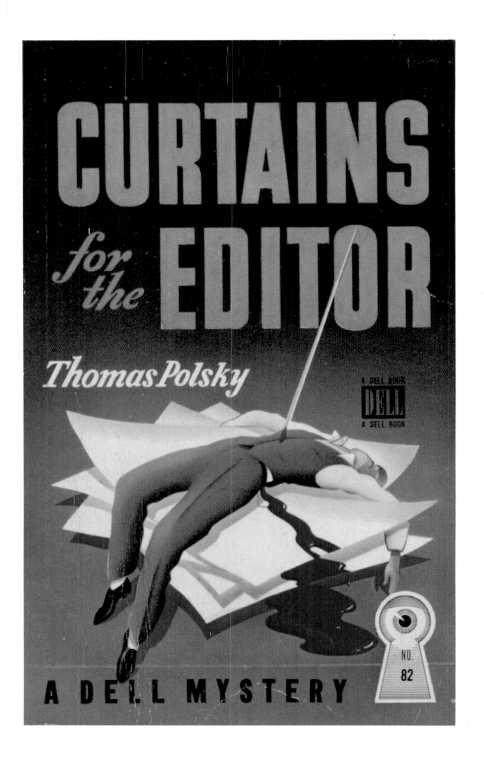

CURTAINS
for the EDITOR

Thomas Polsky

A DELL BOOK
DELL
A DELL BOOK

NO. 82

A DELL MYSTERY

LOVE WAS CHEAP AND LIFE WAS HIGH • Collier Books
Copyright © 1990 by Barry Jay Kaplan

Curtains for the Editor by Thomas Polsky. Published by Dell in 1945. Originally published in hardcover by Dutton in 1939. Cover art by Gerald Gregg, who worked with an airbrush and called his style "a combination of graphic design and stylized realism." Things this mystery is about: "a spindle, a warm half-pint of cream, sugar cookies, a sliver of glass, a flat tire, a brown leather wastebasket, a balcony and Gladys Marlen, full-breasted, full-hipped and full-thighed."